Whole Language Units
for
Holidays

Written by Sandra Merrick

Illustrated by Sue Fullam, Keith Vasconcelles, and Cheryl Buhler

Teacher Created Materials, Inc.
P.O. Box 1214
Huntington Beach, CA 92647
© 1992 Teacher Created Materials, Inc.
Made in U.S.A.

ISBN-1-55734-019-6

Table of Contents

Introduction

The purpose of whole language is to teach children how to read. In *Whole Language Units for Holidays,* children learn to read using activities based on an original story or poem for each holiday. They also learn to enjoy and understand what they read. Students who are not ready to read will learn phonics, appreciate literature, hear rhyme and rhythm, acquire concepts, and understand language structure. They also use thinking skills to analyze, classify, and create while learning to read.

Each unit in this book begins with an original story or poem and includes some or all of the following activities:

- sample lesson plans
- flannel board patterns
- riddles
- art projects
- games
- creative writing
- center ideas
- word banks
- reproducible little books
- phonics activities
- literature

Use as many of these activities as you feel appropriate to meet the needs of your class. Whether you choose to use just the patterns provided or the entire unit, enjoy them.

What Is Whole Language?

In whole language, skills and activities are arranged around a literary experience. For example, children learn the sound of the letter 'B' after they study a poem about black bats. The teacher emphasizes that learning the 'B' sound will help them learn to read words like black and bat. Reading, language, writing, spelling, and speaking are not taught in separate units, but are related to a particular book, story, or poem.

Meaning is emphasized in whole language, but not by asking a few questions about the story. The class is immersed in meaning by repeated experiences with the story or poem (discussions, art, sequencing, cloze, etc.). It is acceptable and desirable for students to memorize the story. When possible, students should act out or "play" the stories.

In whole language, students usually use trade books or Big Books. Vocabulary is not introduced and defined before reading the story. The story is read first for enjoyment. Various activities follow this initial reading.

Creative writing is an important part of whole language. Children use ideas or patterns from the story to create new stories. Younger children will need lots of direction, modeling, and suggestions from the teacher.

Students use approximate or invented spelling during creative writing. Students are urged not to worry about correct spelling, but to sound out the word and spell it the best they can. Spelling correction may intimidate very young writers. Older students can correct and edit a second draft.

Children are immersed in print in a whole language classroom. Walls and bulletin boards are covered with labeled pictures and student's creative writing. Copies of literature and Big Books are available in a reading corner. Copies of books "written" by the students are included.

Whole language emphasizes the process of learning rather than the end product. Each student is at a different place in the learning process. Teachers should take care to treat each student as an individual.

Presenting a Whole Language Unit

There are several ways of presenting whole language units. General suggestions are given below. Each holiday unit has its own sample lesson plan.

- **Introduce the unit.** Activities that involve creative thinking skills are best. Examples of these include brainstorming, associating the new story with past experiences, and making predictions.

- **Present the poem or story using flannel board, magnetic board, chart, or Big Book.** Repeat the story each day varying the method for interest.

- **Make a classroom book for the children to read.** See page 6 for one way to do this.

- **Choose specific skills to work on each day** such as beginning sounds, vocabulary, or rhyming words.

- **Copy the little books**, one for each child. Make a tape of the story or poem to use in a listening center. Students may take the small books home to share with their families.

- **Use cloze sentences** (missing word) from the story to emphasize meaning. This is easy to do on an overhead by using an index card to cover a word.

- **Make word rings.** Use 3" x 5" index cards, book rings, and a hole punch. Copy the selected word onto a card, punch a hole near the corner, and put the card onto a book ring. Add as many cards as you wish to create personalized word rings.

- **Extend the story ideas and characters into centers.** Make an additional set of flannel board figures for play. Use stick puppets or headbands to act out the story. Provide a script.

- **Use patterns or ideas** from the story for creative writing.

Using the Patterns

For each of the stories or poems in this book, patterns of the characters and props are provided. Suggestions for making and using these patterns follow.

Traditional Felt Figures

Trace the patterns onto felt squares, which can be purchased in craft, department, or fabric stores. Use very sharp scissors to cut. Attach pieces to each other using an extra heavy tacky craft or fabric glue. Include movable eyes (6mm size) and tiny pom pom noses (6 mm), if desired. Word cards to match the figures can be made from 1 ½" x 5" rectangles of heavy nonwoven smooth fabric interfacing. (Pellon 930® works well for this.) These will adhere easily to flannel boards. Then print the word with a fine point permanent marker. Use the felt figures and words to act out stories on the flannel board. Make two sets, one for the teacher and one for the children. Encourage children to make up their own stories using the figures.

Quick Color-and-Cut Figures

Copy, color, and cut out the patterns in this book. Seek help from students, volunteer parents, and aides. Many copiers will copy on heavy stock like index, tag, or construction paper. These papers can be purchased in many sizes, including the standard 8 ½" x 11". (Patterns can also be duplicated onto wallpaper samples cut to fit the copier. This eliminates coloring, since only the features need to be highlighted with markers to make delightful, stuffed-animal-like figures.) Laminate. Glue squares of felt, to the back for flannel board use. Attach magnetic strips (available from craft stores) for use on magnetic boards. Dry under a heavy book.

Figures for Overhead

Figures made from felt or paper can sometimes be used directly on the overhead if their outlines are distinct enough for easy identification. You may wish to use a copy machine or have a copy shop make overhead transparencies of the patterns and/or the little books. These can be colored with transparency pens. This provides another way to use the patterns for storytelling and instruction.

Using the Patterns *(cont.)*

Fabric Interfacing Flannel Board Figures

Put heavy nonwoven interfacing over the patterns and trace with a permanent marker. Color with crayons. These can be ironed if they become wrinkled.

Puppets and Paper Dolls

Give each child copies of the patterns to color, cut out, and glue to craft sticks for their own stick puppets. For a teacher set, copy the patterns onto heavy paper and laminate before taping to craft sticks. Place a set of the laminated, colored figures (without craft sticks) in a paper doll center for children's use. Encourage the children to make new clothes and accessories for the figures.

Bulletin Boards

Enlarge the patterns to make related bulletin boards. Use an opaque projector if you wish to make really large pieces. Otherwise, you may wish to simply enlarge on a copy machine.

To Make a Big Book

Make a Big Book to present the story or for the children to read in centers (A good size to use is ¼ of a large poster board). Copy the text of the story or poem, a few lines on each page. Draw pictures or use a copy machine to enlarge patterns from this book; cut, color, and glue to pages. Or, have the children illustrate the pages. For the easiest Big Book of all, use a copy machine to enlarge the little book pages to desired size.

To Assemble Little Books

Have copies of the little book pages made for each child. During class have the students color and cut the little books. Show them how to put the pages in order, then staple. Give them the opportunity to illustrate the cover and color the pictures. Let the students keep the little books at school for a few days, using them for some of the suggested activities. Then let them take the little books home.

Art Projects

You can also use the patterns for art projects. Make copies and glue them onto stiff paper. Students may trace, color, cut, and glue to create their own pictures.

Holiday Centers

Much learning takes place in centers. Games and center activities are as important as shared reading. Create your own centers as you see a need they may fill.

Reading Center with Flannel Board

Put a flannel board or magnetic board in a center. For each holiday, make an additional set of flannel board figures for the children to play with. Make corresponding 1 1/2" x 5" nonwoven interfacing word cards for the children to match with the flannel board figures. A fine point permanent marker writes very well on interfacing. Leave a copy of each piece of holiday literature ("Black, Black"; "Five Wild Turkeys"; "Is It Christmas Yet?"; "Where Is Holly Heart?"; "The Bunny School") for the children to use with the flannel pieces.

Make this area cozy, comfortable, and accessible. Stock with a large variety of holiday story books. Have books on different reading levels, including picture books and wordless books. Include both commercial and student-authored books. Put books on shelves or in baskets. A cleanable bean bag chair and/or pillow are a welcome addition to the reading center.

Post a copy of the holiday word bank found in each unit. Children can use it and their word rings to practice unit vocabulary and write their own stories.

Listening Center

Use a blank tape and record your own version of each piece of holiday literature. Make the little books for each unit so students can follow along in their own copies. Record the holiday riddles. Make copies of the riddles for students to follow as they listen to them. Read holiday stories onto tapes and provide the books for students to follow. Store the books and tapes separately, encouraging students to read and match titles of books, and cassette tape labels when they are making a listening choice.

Block Center

Provide blocks of various shapes and sizes. Encourage students to use them to build appropriate holiday structures such as haunted houses, turkey pens, or a bunny school. Use the patterns to make posterboard or laminated tagboard figures. Students can use them as paper dolls along with their block creations to act out their own holiday stories.

Blocks can also be used to make a small stage on a table so the children can use stick puppets to retell the stories and poems.

Math Center

Make felt figures for the children to use as manipulatives. Encourage them to create patterns with the figures, to make up story word problems, and to use them to help solve simple addition and subtraction problems.

Black, Black!

Black, black!
What is black?
Black is a witch's hat.

Black, black!
What is black?
Black is a Halloween cat.

Black, black!
What is black?
Black is a scary bat.

Black, black!
What is black?
Black is when you turn off the light.

Black, black!
What is black?
Black is a moonless night.

Black, black!
What is black?
Black is a Halloween fright.

8

Sample Lessons

Each of the suggested lessons can take from one to several days to complete.

Note: Prepare flannel board figures before presenting the unit. See pages 5 and 6 for quick and easy ways to do this.

Day 1: Before reading the poem "Black, Black!" brainstorm with the class. On the chalkboard write: Halloween is a _____. Tell the children to think of Halloween things. Record these on the chalkboard. Include all suggestions. Then go back and erase all the words that do not belong. Read over the words. Use them to complete the sentence "Halloween is a _____." Explain that they have created a poem. After class, transfer the poem to a chart or class book.

Present the poem "Black, Black!" (page 8). Students should memorize and "read" it. Use it with the flannel board figures. Patterns are found on pages 11-18. Hold up each figure as it is presented in the poem. After reading "Black, Black!" ask if it had any of the same Halloween words as the class poem. Find the words common to both poems.

Sing a Halloween phonics song to the tune of "Farmer in the Dell." As you sing, add characters to the flannel board. Example:

Bat starts with b.
Bat starts with b.
Hi, ho the dairio.
Bat starts with b.   *(Add a bat to the flannel board.)*

Have children make up their own verses, adding new Halloween words.

Do the Witch Drawing Lesson on page 20. Children may do this individually on their own paper or on a chalkboard. Enlarge each section and mount on tag or poster board. Hang it near a chalkboard that the children use so they may copy it.

Day 2: Repeat the poem using an overhead. Most flannel board figures work on the overhead. Cut 2 squares of black construction paper. In one square punch several holes and use it for a "moonless night." (The holes serve as stars.) In the other square, punch 2 larger holes for eyes and use it for "turn out the light."

Follow up with riddles (page 19). As you read them and students guess the answers, put the figure on the flannel board. Add a word card made from interfacing to review each Halloween word. Discuss each one. (This would be a good time to give directions for the Fabulous Folder game, page 21, since they are similar.)

Sample Lessons *(cont.)*

Review the Halloween phonics song from Day 1.

Make word cards for "Black, Black!" on 3" x 5" index cards. Pass them out. Let students come up and match their word card to the word on the flannel board. To make this activity more challenging, remove the word cards from the flannel board. Point to a figure and say, "Do you have the word for witch?" Let the student who has the correct word come up and place it on the board.

Day 3: Use a Big Book, classroom book, or transparencies of the little book pages to practice reading the poem again. Make sentence strips and use in a pocket chart.

Make word rings. (See page 4.) Use some of the words from the word bank (page 24). Work with a small group while others work in centers. Read the poem "Black, Black!" Ask the students which words they would like to learn. Punch a hole in each card and place on the student's individual word ring. Students can keep word rings in their desks to practice writing, reading, and other activities. Make more cards as needed.

Extend into center activities. (See page 7.) Students select at which center they would like to work.

Do some cloze exercises. Cloze is another word for missing word or words. Copy parts of the poem on the chalkboard. Rhyming words make the missing words more predictable. Example:

> **Black, black!**
> **What is black?**
> **Black is a witch's _____.**

Repeat with the other verses, putting blanks for "cat" and "bat." This exercise can be made more difficult by leaving out other words or more words. Do orally as a class.

Day 4: Let each child make a little book. Reproduce pages 25-28 for each child. Cut on the dotted lines. Check to make certain the pages are in the correct order. Staple the books together. Students color the little books, making sure colors are consistent with the text. Read the books repeatedly in class. Let students take the little books home to share with parents.

Choose a creative writing activity. There are several suggestions given on page 23. Do some Halloween math using the flannel board. Use the lesson given on page 31.

Day 5: Complete the Black, Black! Picture Match (page 29). Discuss the difference between real and make-believe. Make a chart with the two categories, and let children brainstorm to fill it in. Follow up with the Real or Make Believe worksheet (page 30).

As a culminating activity have a Halloween costume parade. Encourage children to dress in costumes of characters from "Black, Black!"

Patterns

Patterns (cont.)

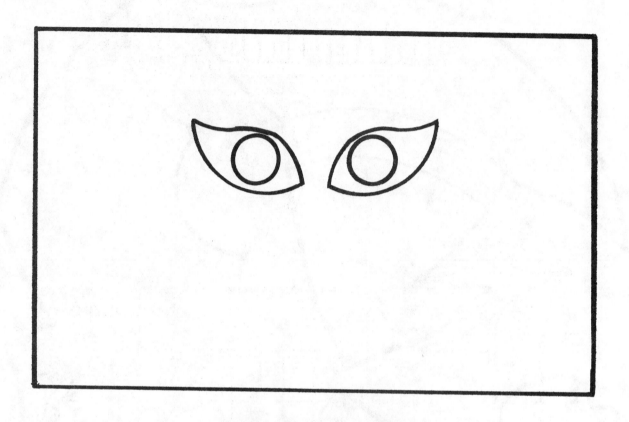

Patterns *(cont.)*

Patterns (cont.)

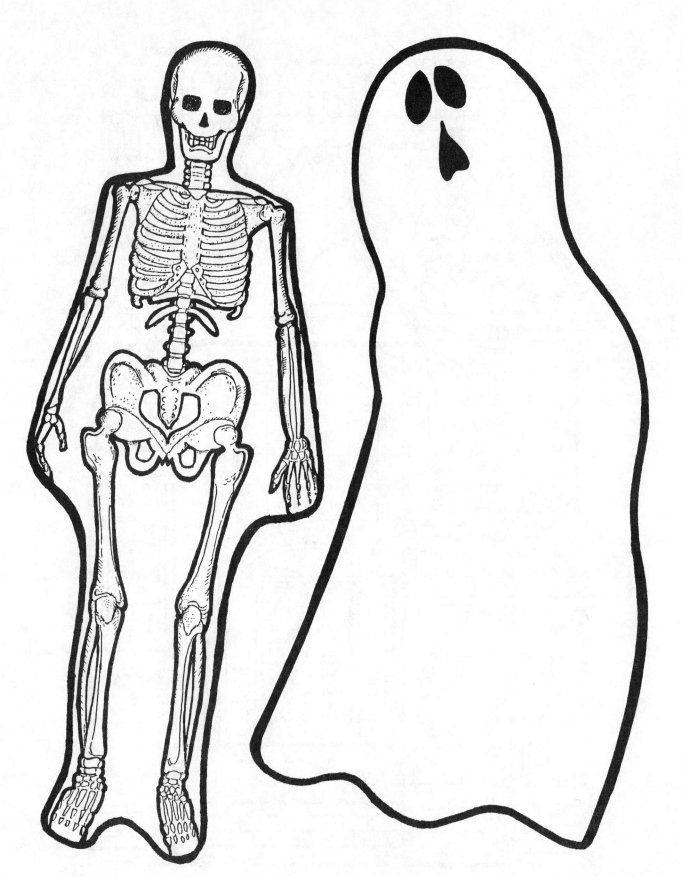

Patterns *(cont.)*

Patterns (cont.)

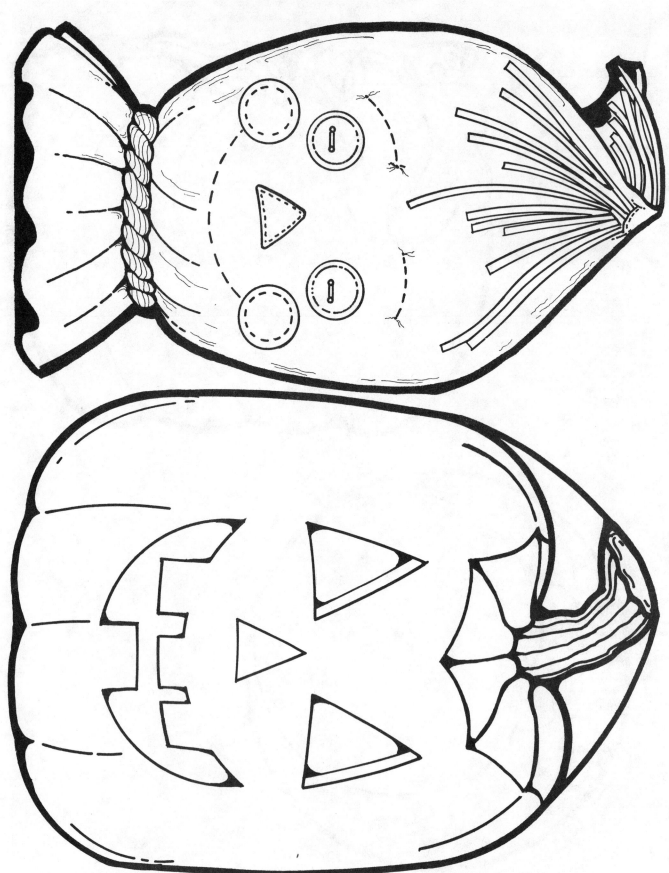

16

Patterns *(cont.)*

Patterns *(cont.)*

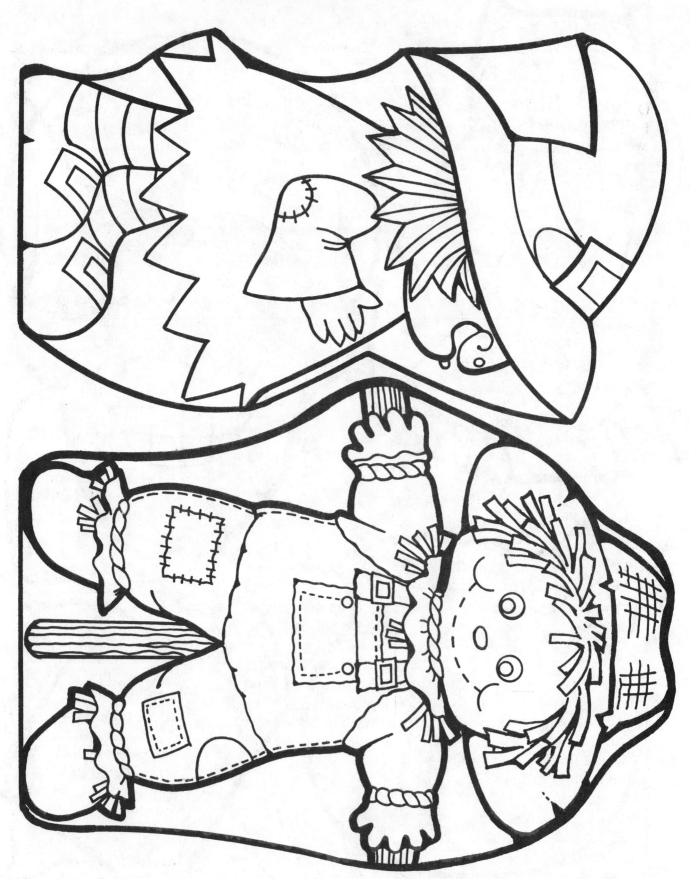

18

Halloween Riddles

Use these riddles along with flannel board figures. They are an excellent way to teach inference to young children.

Out of the graveyard,
Filled with stones,
No hair or skin;
I'm nothing but bones.
What am I?
(skeleton)

My hat is black.
My face is green.
My laugh is mean.
I ride a broom
On Halloween.
What am I?
(witch)

The shadows chase the sun away.
The stars come out to dance and play.
I'm at the end of another day.
What am I?
(night)

I fly at night.
I hunt by sound.
I live in a cave.
And sleep upside down.
People are scared;
They shouldn't be.
I eat mice and bugs.
Please don't hurt me.
What am I?
(bat)

I grew on a vine,
Right on the ground.
I have a big smile,
All orange and round.
What am I?
(Jack-o-Lantern)

My door is gone.
My windows cracked.
Ghosts float through walls
And then float back.
You hear strange noises,
Bam, bang, and whack.
What am I?
(haunted house)

My eyes are gold.
My fur is black.
I hiss and spit
And arch my back.
My claws are sharp.
I might attack.
What am I?
(Halloween cat)

I like to stay
Just out of sight.
If you see me,
I might be white.
I float through houses
In the black of night.
What am I?
(ghost)

Witch Drawing Lesson

Follow these steps to draw a witch. Practice drawing on another piece of paper. You may want to change the hair or the face. Use your crayons to add color.

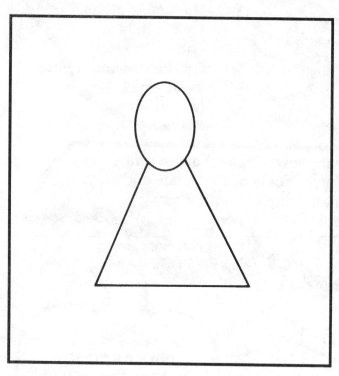

Fabulous Folder Game

Use this phonics game for Halloween. Adapt it to work for other holidays by using patterns found throughout this book.

- Glue 8 library pockets inside an orange file folder for Halloween.
- Color and cut out the figures on page 22. Glue one on each pocket.
- Decorate the folder cover by letting children color, cut Halloween figures and glue them on. Label the cover Halloween Phonics.
- Glue two library pockets to the back cover for storage.
- Laminate over the pictures and pockets. Slit each pocket open.
- Insert 3" x 5" index cards into the pockets. Use a marker to write a lower case letter on the part of the card that shows above the library pocket. Example: Write 'w' on the card in the witch pocket. (Orange index cards are available. Color coding makes for easy clean up.)

Children can play the game by placing the card with the beginning sound that matches the picture in each pocket. As a variation, write the entire word on an index card.

Fabulous Folder Game (cont.)

See page 21 for suggested use of these patterns.

Creative Writing
Using Language Patterns

Make a Big Book or a classroom book. Read Bill Martin's *Brown Bear, Brown Bear* (Henry Holt, 1983). Use the pattern in this book to write a Halloween Big Book with your class. Start with "Old house, old house, what do you see?" Review Halloween words. Then ask, "What kind of witch do you want? Should she be old, green, and ugly?" Explain what nouns are, and help the children select some. Explain adjectives and select them. Laminate and bind with book rings.

The following phrases can be used to start pages in individual or class books: Old house; Jack-O-Lantern; Dark night; White ghost; Full moon; Scarecrow; Brown bat; Green witch.

The last sentence may be "I see Halloween looking at me."

Listening

What do witches eat? Read stories to the class such as *Bony-Legs* by Joanna Cole (Scholastic, 1988) and *Baba Yaga* by Ernest Small and Blair Lent (Houghton Mifflin). Have them listen to records like Hap Palmer's "Witch's Brew"and Golden Records' Halloween album, "Witch's Stew." Try to list all the things that witches eat. Be sure to mention words like stew and brew. Then use this pattern to write a poem.

A witch eats_____.

A witch eats stew.

A witch eats _____.

A witch drinks brew.

Better watch out!

She might eat you!

New Poems from Old

Use the pattern from "Black, Black!" It does not have to rhyme.

_____, _____.

What is _____?

_____ is a _____.

Use other color words in the blanks. Example:

Green, green.

What is green?

Green is a bean.

Word Bank

A word bank is a collection of related words. It should grow and be added to as children learn more about the topic being studied. Use the words below to begin a Halloween word bank that students can contribute to as studies progress. Use the words from the Halloween word bank to create Halloween word rings. This is a quick, fun way for students to integrate reading and writing. (See page 4 for directions to make word rings.) Although students are allowed to choose the words they want to put on their word rings, their choices can be easily influenced by the teacher. For instance, if the teacher displays the ghost flannel board figure after reading a poem about a ghost, it is easy to predict what word most of the children will choose.

Suggested Words for Halloween Word Bank

cat	house	monster
bat	ghost	snake
rat	witch	Halloween
hat	green	broom
sat	boo	people
fat	good	mean
night	bad	ugly
moon	vampire	haunted

24

Making Little Books

My Little Book
of
"Black, Black!"

_____
Name

Black, black!
What is black?
Black is a witch's hat

1

Making Little Books *(cont.)*

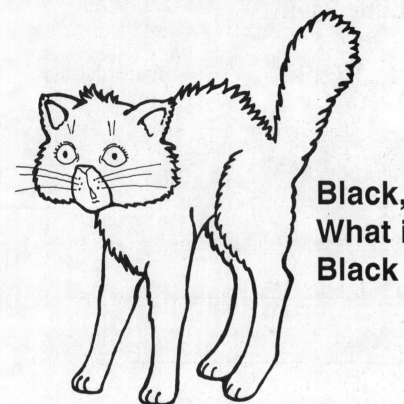

Black, black!
What is black?
Black is a Halloween cat.

2

Black, black!
What is black?
Black is a scary bat.

3

Making Little Books *(cont.)*

Black, black!
What is black?
Black is when you turn off the light. 4

Black, black!
What is black?
Black is a moonless night. 5

Making Little Books *(cont.)*

Black, black!
What is black?
Black is a Halloween fright.

6

**The End
of
Black, Black!**

28

Making Little Books

"Black, Black!" Picture Match

Directions: Color pictures. Cut on dotted lines. Glue the picture beside the correct word.

cat		
bat		
hat		
night		
light		

Real or Make Believe?

Circle the things that are real.   Put an X on the things that are make-believe.

Flannel Board Math

The flannel board is the ideal medium for math. Use the flannel board figures in this unit to help solve the problems below. Let children try writing some of their own.

Enlarge and reduce patterns (pages 11-18) as necessary. See directions for using the patterns, pages 5-6. Make flannel board letters and numbers by drawing them onto squares of felt or using stencils as a template to trace and cut them out, or let a child hold up a tagboard numeral card instead.

How Many Ghosts in the Haunted House?

Preparation: Make a felt haunted house, felt numerals, and several felt ghosts. Place the haunted house and a numeral at the bottom of the flannel board. Lay several felt ghosts on the table in front of the flannel board.

Ask the children, "Can someone read the numeral and put up the correct number to show how many ghosts came out of the haunted house?" Repeat, using other numerals.

The Halloween Parade

Preparation: Make a window with a dark sky (page 12) and a variety of flannel board characters (witch, scarecrow, cat, bat, etc.). Make a set of flannel board numerals. Place the window with the dark sky at the bottom of the flannel board. Near the top, put a variety of flannel board characters. Lay the numerals on the table in front of the flannel board.

Tell this story to the children. *A little boy looked out his window and saw a Halloween parade. How many creatures were in the parade?* Have them come up and select the appropriate numeral. Continue by adding the skeleton, jack-o-lantern, and ghost, or remove Halloween figures.

Party Decorations

Preparation: Make 8 ghosts (4 white, and 4 of another color) for counting and patterning activities.

Tell the children this story. *Willa Witch was putting up Halloween decorations for her party.* (Place a witch figure at bottom of the flannel board.) *She hung pictures of ghosts along the walls: white, yellow, white, yellow _____.* Put up ghosts in a 2-color pattern. Ask if anyone can come up and help Willa finish the pattern. Put felt ghosts on the table near the flannel board. Then ask if anyone can think up a new pattern.

Variations: Alternate jack-o-lanterns with ghosts. On another day, repeat the lesson using a three color pattern.

Five Wild Turkeys

A farmer and his wife caught five wild turkeys and put them inside a tall pen. They wanted to eat the turkeys for Thanksgiving. They were going to invite their family and all their friends. But they forgot that wild turkeys can fly very well. When the turkeys saw the ax, they just flew away.

Five wild turkeys
Locked in a pen.
They can't fly out,
But they tried again.

Three wild turkeys
Don't know what to do.
One flew out,
Then there were two.

Five wild turkeys
Pushed on the door.
One flew out,
Then there were four.

Two wild turkeys
This is no fun.
One flew out,
Then there was one.

Four wild turkeys
Sad as can be.
One flew out,
Then there were three.

One wild turkey
That's not many.
He flew out,
Then there weren't any.

They flew to a tree
And slept all night.
The cook couldn't find them,
And that's all right.

Sample Lessons

Each of the lessons suggested can take from one to several days to complete.

Note: Before introducing the story, make the figures found on pages 35-39 into flannel or magnetic figures. See pages 5-6 for directions.

Day 1: Before reading "Five Wild Turkeys," give the students some background information. Look in encyclopedias and magazines for pictures of both domestic and wild turkeys. Both *Your Big Backyard* and *Ranger Rick* magazines (published by National Wildlife Federation, 8925 Leesburg Pike, Vienna, VA 22184-0001) are excellent resources. Point out the differences between domestic and wild turkeys, such as coloration and where they live. This is an excellent time to introduce the concept of endangered species. In many areas of the country, wild turkeys have been hunted to extinction. The National Forestry Service is raising wild turkeys and releasing them back into the forests. Read "Five Wild Turkeys." Explain that the setting for this story is a farm. Ask children to name some farm animals. As each animal is named, place it on a flannel or magnetic board. Discuss what it does on the farm.

Follow up with a poem. Read "Gobble, Gobble" found in *It's Thanksgiving* by Jack Prelutsky (Greenwillow, 1982). Write the words "gobble" and "turkey" on the chalkboard. Discuss the words.

Day 2: Do some turkey art. Let children do a hand turkey. Children put one of their hands onto a piece of paper, spreading their fingers out. Using a crayon, they trace around each finger. Their thumb becomes the turkey's face. They need to add feet, an eye, a beak, and a wattle.

Reread "Five Wild Turkeys." If there is no time to make a Big Book or a classroom book, copy the little book pages (pages 44-47) and make transparencies for the overhead. Read through it twice. On the second reading, pass out large cards with the numerals 1,2,3,4,5 on them to five children. Have them stand in front of the room. As each number is read in the poem, have that child sit down or fly away to another part of the room.

Teach a lesson on farm phonics using the figures on pages 35-39. Using flannel, magnetic, or interfacing word cards with letters, show the children how to match the figure to the beginning letter. Extend this game into the flannel board center. Sing a turkey phonics song with the students to the tune of "London Bridge."

> **Turkey always starts with t,**
> **Starts with t,**
> **Starts with t.**
> **Turkey always starts with t,**
> **The first letter.**

Repeat with other animals. Use the figures you have previously made and let students place them on the flannel or magnetic board as each verse is sung.

Sample Lessons*(cont.)*

Day 3: Repeat the story. Have children make the little books on pages 44-47. See page 6 for directions on making little books. On the first page, have children write their names and illustrate. Let them read the story and take the books home.

Make word rings. Use the words found in the word bank on page 42. Use them during center time.

Day 4: Make a Shape Turkey. Use the pattern on page 41. Give each child pieces of orange and brown construction paper and a scrap of red. From the brown paper make two rectangles for feathers, and the large brown circle for the body. From the orange make two rectangles for feathers, the head, the beak, and two feet. Use the red to cut the oval for the wattle. Have children assemble the turkey, drawing in the details.

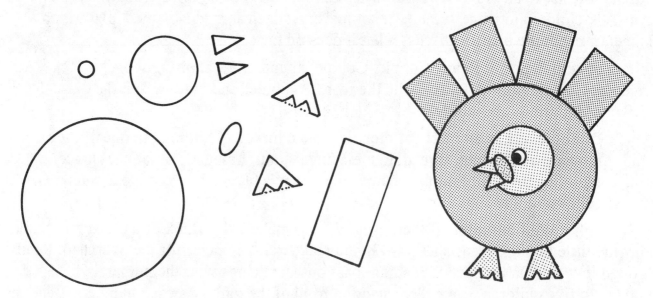

Talk about Thanksgiving customs. Share the history of Thanksgiving with the class. Let children describe how their families spend the day. What do they eat? With the class create a Marvelous Menu that includes lots of description such as "golden, brown, juicy, stuffed turkey." Give the children paper plates and have them draw what their Thanksgiving plate would look like.

Day 5: Do some turkey math. See page 48 for suggestions.

Make a counting book using the "Turkeys Wild" poem. See page 43 for directions. Let each child illustrate.

As a culminating activity have the students act out "Five Wild Turkeys." Parts include the farmer, his wife, and the five turkeys. Make name tags out of construction paper or use the patterns and yarn with characters' names to hang around students' necks. Let students help make scenery and props such as the ax, a tree, and a turkey pen. The teacher can narrate or have students without parts read the story chorally.

Patterns

Patterns *(cont.)*

Patterns *(cont.)*

Patterns *(cont.)*

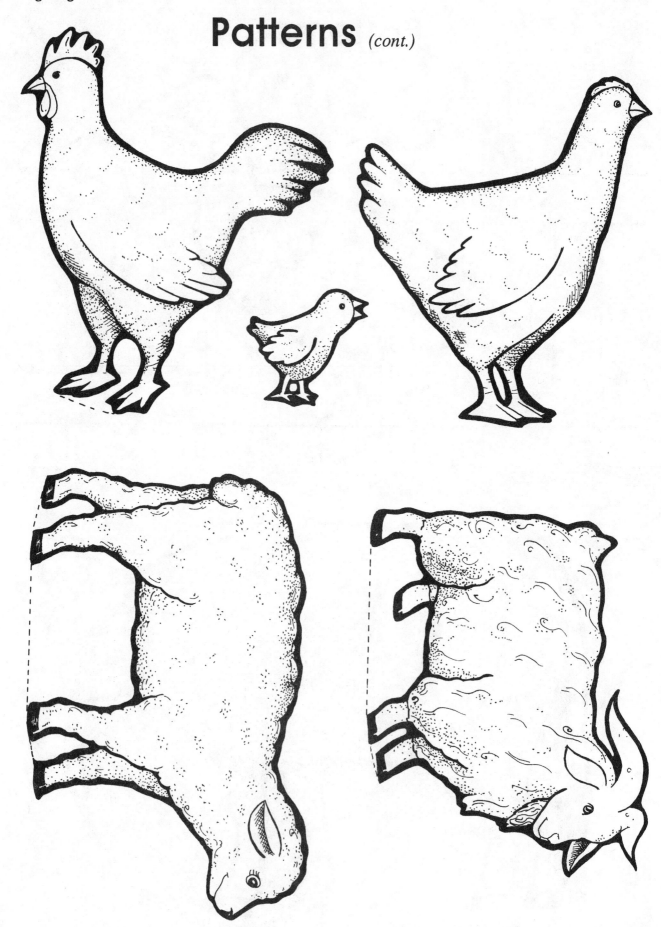

38

Patterns *(cont.)*

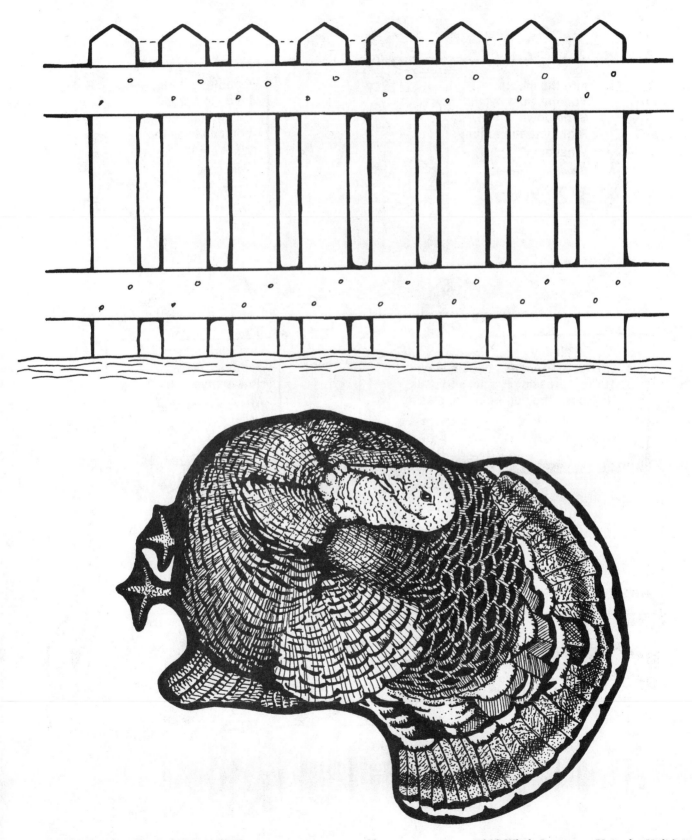

Thanksgiving Riddles

Use these riddles along with flannel board figures. They are an excellent way to teach inference to young children.

Into the mouth,
Yummy, yummy, yummy;
Slide down, down, down,
Right into the tummy.
What am I?
(food)

Gobble, gobble, gobble;
I hide in a tree.
Behind fall leaves,
You can't see me.
What am I?
(wild turkey)

We eat all day.
Grandpa, Grandma, cousin May;
Turkey, dressing, yams, and peas;
Now pass the pumpkin pie, please.
What day is it?
(Thanksgiving)

Five wild turkeys.
One flies away.
How many are left?
What do you say?
(four)

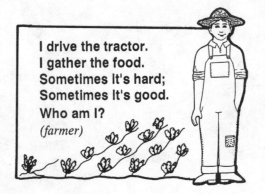

I drive the tractor.
I gather the food.
Sometimes it's hard;
Sometimes it's good.
Who am I?
(farmer)

40

Shape Turkey

*See page 34 for directions.

Word Bank

A word bank is a collection of related words. It should grow and be added to as children learn more about the topic being studied. Suggested words for this work bank are taken from the Thanksgiving season and the story "Five Wild Turkeys." Encourage children to add other words.

The word "night" also appears in the Halloween Word Bank (page 24). This provides a good opportunity to review and study rhyming words.

Use the words from the Thanksgiving word bank to create Thanksgiving word rings. This is a quick, fun way for students to integrate reading and writing. (See page 4 for directions to make word rings.)

Use the words below to begin a Thanksgiving word bank that students can contribute to as studies progress.

Suggested Words for Thanksgiving Word Bank

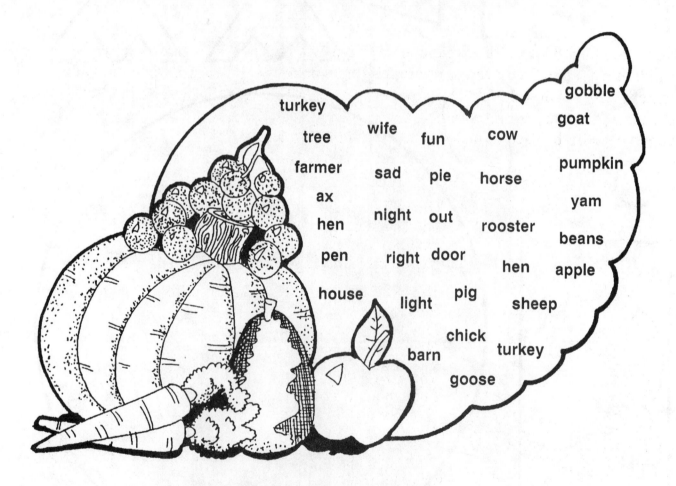

Creative Writing

Use these creative writing ideas throughout the Thanksgiving unit.

Food Vocabulary

Let children look through magazines and cut out food pictures. With the class, look at several pictures and name the food. Talk about the beginning sounds. Have each child select his/her favorite food picture, and glue it onto a sheet of construction paper. Under the picture write, "I like_____" (fill in the name of the food). The child will copy the sentence under the teacher's sentence. Select two other food pictures and do the same. Have the children make a book cover from construction paper. Write the title "My Food Book" on the chalkboard for the children to copy.

Farm Animal Sentence Pattern

On 4 or 5 sentence strips, write, "I see a _____." Place them in a pocket chart. Read the strips and ask the children to think of farm animals. Use the patterns (pages 35-39) to make felt or tag animals to use in the pocket chart to make a rebus.

Turkey Counting Book

Make counting books. Reverse the turkey rhyme and begin with one turkey. Let children write there own verses or use the verses below. Use the same pattern to add turkeys rather than subtract them. Copy the verses below onto five 8 ½" x 11" sheets of paper. Add a construction paper cover. Staple together. Let the children illustrate. The verses can also be used to make a class Counting Big Book.

Turkeys Wild

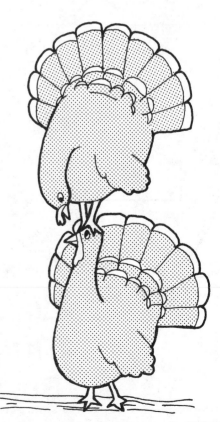

One wild turkey
Alone and blue
One turkey joins it,
Now there are two.

Two wild turkeys
Sitting in a tree.
One turkey joins them.
Now there are three.

Three wild turkeys
Find an apple core.
One turkey joins them.
Now there are four.

Four wild turkeys
Glad to be alive.
One turkey joins them.
Now there are five.

Making Little Books

My Little Book

of

Five Wild Turkeys

_____

Name

Five wild turkeys
Locked in a pen.
They can't fly out,
But they tried again.

1

Making Little Books *(cont.)*

**Five wild turkeys
Pushed on the door.
One flew out,
Then there were four.**   **2**

**Four wild turkeys

Sad as can be.

One flew out,

Then there were three.**   **3**

Making Little Books (cont.)

- -

Three wild turkeys
Don't know what to do.
One flew out,
Then there were two.

4

- -

Two wild turkeys
This is no fun.
One flew out,
Then there was one.

5

- -

Making Little Books *(cont.)*

One wild turkey
That's not many.
He flew out,
Then there weren't any.

6

They flew to a tree
And slept all night.
The cook couldn't find them,
And that's all right.

7

Flannel Board Turkey Math

Preparation: Make or purchase felt numerals 1-10, 10 small felt circles, 5 large felt circles, and 8 or 10 of each of the animal figures.

Counting Bowls

Put 5 turkeys on the flannel board. Let the farmer's wife (a child) count the turkeys to see how many bowls she will need to feed them. Then clip a piece of paper over the turkeys with a clothespin. Place a set of 7 or more small bowls (felt circles) in a pile in front of flannel board. Look to see if the child counts to 5, or if he/she puts out all the bowls. This is a good evaluation procedure. Then uncover the turkeys and let the student match the bowls to the turkeys. Repeat this activity several times by changing the numbers each time.

Sets to Match Numerals

Place the numeral 6 on the flannel board and 8 small circles in a pile in front of the flannel board. Do not read the numeral to the student. Explain that he/she has a job on the farm. Point to the 6 and say that the farmer left him/her a note to feed this many goats. Have the student put the correct number of bowls on the flannel board near the numeral. Have another child check the work by reading the numeral and counting the bowls aloud. This is also a good evaluation to see if the child stops counting at 6 or if he/she keeps counting to 8. Repeat with other children, hanging the numeral and the animals to be fed. They can feed 3 cats, 5 horses, 7 turkeys, 4 cows, etc.

Same Number

Place 5 small circles (bowls) close together in a cluster at the bottom of the flannel board. Put the 5 turkeys far apart across the top of the flannel board. Ask the children if there are more bowls or more turkeys. (This is a "trick" question.) Take at least 4 predictions. Let a child feed the turkeys by matching bowls to turkeys. Then ask the question again and have the child explain his/her answer. Reverse the process by putting the turkeys close together and the bowls far apart.

Fatten Them Up

Place 5 turkeys very close together. Explain that the turkeys were too thin, so the farmer's wife got bigger bowls. Replace the 5 small circles with 5 large circles. Now, are there more turkeys or more bowls? Take predictions. Then let someone feed the turkeys by moving 1 turkey to each bowl. Ask the child to explain his/her answer. This is a good opportunity to explain that size isn't important when counting things. The question "Which is bigger?" is not the same question as "How many?" If you compare 5 elephants and 5 mice, you will have the same number, but not the same size.

Is It Christmas Yet?

One day I found a Christmas card.
"Mama! Mama!" I said,
"Is it Christmas yet?"
"Not yet," said Mama.
So I put it in the closet, and I waited.

One day I found a candy cane.
"Mama! Mama!" I said,
"Is it Christmas yet?"
"Not yet," said Mama.
So I put it in the closet, and I waited.

One day I found a Christmas present.
"Mama! Mama!" I said,
"Is it Christmas yet?"
"Not yet," said Mama.
So I put it in the closet, and I waited.

One day I found a Christmas tree.
"Mama! Mama!" I said,
"Is it Christmas yet?"
"Not yet," said Mama.
So I put it in the closet, and I waited.

Is It Christmas Yet? *(cont.)*

One day I found a reindeer.
"Mama! Mama!" I said,
"Is it Christmas yet?"
"Not yet," said Mama.
So I put him in the closet, and I waited.

One day I found an elf.
"Mama! Mama!" I said,
"Is it Christmas yet?"
"Not yet," said Mama.
So I put him in the closet, and I waited.

One day I found Santa.
"Mama! Mama!" I said,
"Is it Christmas yet?"
"Yes," said Mama.

Out came the Christmas card.
Out came the candy cane.
Out came the Christmas present.
Out came the Christmas tree.
Out came the reindeer.
Out came the elf.

"Ho, ho, ho!" said Santa,
and it was Christmas!

Sample Lessons

Each of the lessons suggested can take from one to several days to complete.

Day 1: Prepare your room with a Christmas bulletin board. Use an opaque projector to enlarge the tree pattern on page 64 to bulletin board size. Reproduce several Christmas tree ornaments (page 60) onto red paper. Write words from "Is It Christmas Yet?" on each one. Glue them onto the Christmas tree. Add a Santa's List of Readers. Each day allow a few children to try to read the words on the tree. Those who are successful can have their names put on Santa's list. Use the ornament patterns to make flash cards for children to use at home. Those who cannot read the words can also get on Santa's list by saying the name of the beginning letter and then making the letter sound correctly.

Ask the children to think of Christmas words. Write them on the chalkboard. Be sure the list includes: Santa, snowman, sleigh, star, stocking, snow, elf, present, tree, reindeer, candy cane, Christmas card. As children say words that begin with the letter 's' write them into a separate column. Ask them if they notice something unusual about that column. Ask them to think of any more Christmas words they can they begin with 's.' Add them to the list.

Present "Is It Christmas Yet?" Prepare the patterns on page 53-60, placing each figure on the flannel or magnetic board as you read the story.

Day 2: Reread the story. Make overhead transparencies using the little books (pages 65-69). Follow up with a phonics lesson on the letter 's'. Tie a piece of yarn around the flannel board to divide it into two sections. Present the flannel board figures and discuss beginning sounds. Use the following figures: Santa, snow, snowman, sleigh, star, stocking, elf, tree, and reindeer. Sort the figures into those that begin with 's' and those that do not.

Extend into centers. (See page 7.) Place the flannel board and the sorting by 's' lesson in the flannel board center for the children to practice. Add other felt figures, including a present, a candy cane, and Mama.

Adapt this as a clothespin game. Shrink the patterns for Christmas figures and glue onto posterboard. Color and laminate. Write the letter 's' on several clothespins and have the children clip them to the pictures that begin with 's.'

Sample Lessons *(cont.)*

Day 3: Introduce the words of the story in a Big Book or on the overhead. Read the story twice. Encourage children to join in on the second reading. Compare two pages of the story so that the children can see how similar they are. If you are using the overhead, just place one page on top of the other.

Follow up with Christmas riddles (page 61). Use the flannel board figures after reading each riddle. Then put up a word card for each flannel board figure. Ask the children to learn to read Christmas words.

Let children do the Christmas math activity (page 71).

Day 4: Students color, assemble, and read little books. (See page 6 for directions.) Make a front and back cover by cutting a piece of construction paper in half. Using the little books, play "Find the Word." Tell the children to point to these words on page 1 of their little books: Christmas, Mama, closet, I, and card. Walk around the room to check. On another day, do this same exercise by using small pieces of tag to cover the words on an overhead transparency. If using a big book, words can be covered by using sticky note paper. Ask the children to guess which word is covered. On other pages, look for the words: tree, elf, candy, reindeer, Santa, said, so, and Ho, ho, ho.

Use Picture Match (page 70) for "Is It Christmas Yet?"

Do a drawing lesson for seasonal items such as snowmen, stars, and Santa.

Day 5: Bring in Christmas cards to show the children. Explain that they are sent to friends and family at Christmas time. Write the words "Merry Christmas" on the chalkboard. Pass out red or green construction paper. Have the children fold in half to make a Christmas card. Inside the card, have each child copy "Merry Christmas" and have each sign his/her name. Make a copy of the children's individual school pictures on a copy machine. Cut apart and distribute to the children to glue on the cover. Decorate the cover with glue and glitter. This is an easy Christmas gift to give parents.

As a culminating activity, invite a group from a senior center or visit one and have the children read "Is It Christmas Yet?" Let them read in groups, one being "I" the other being "Mama."

Patterns

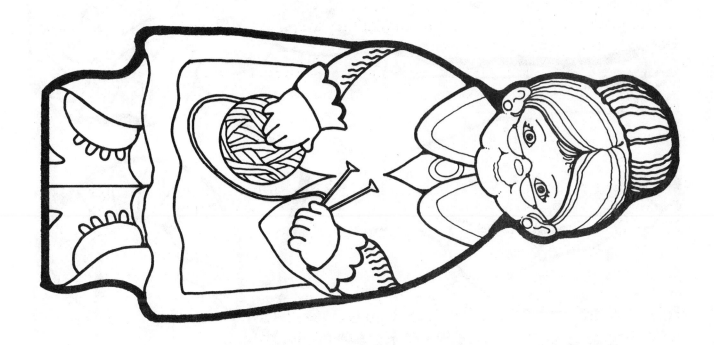

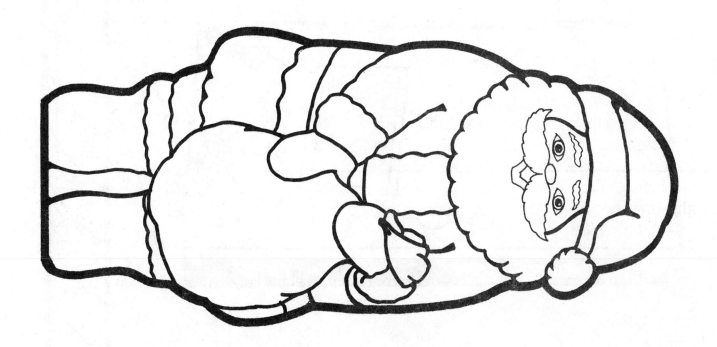

Patterns *(cont.)*

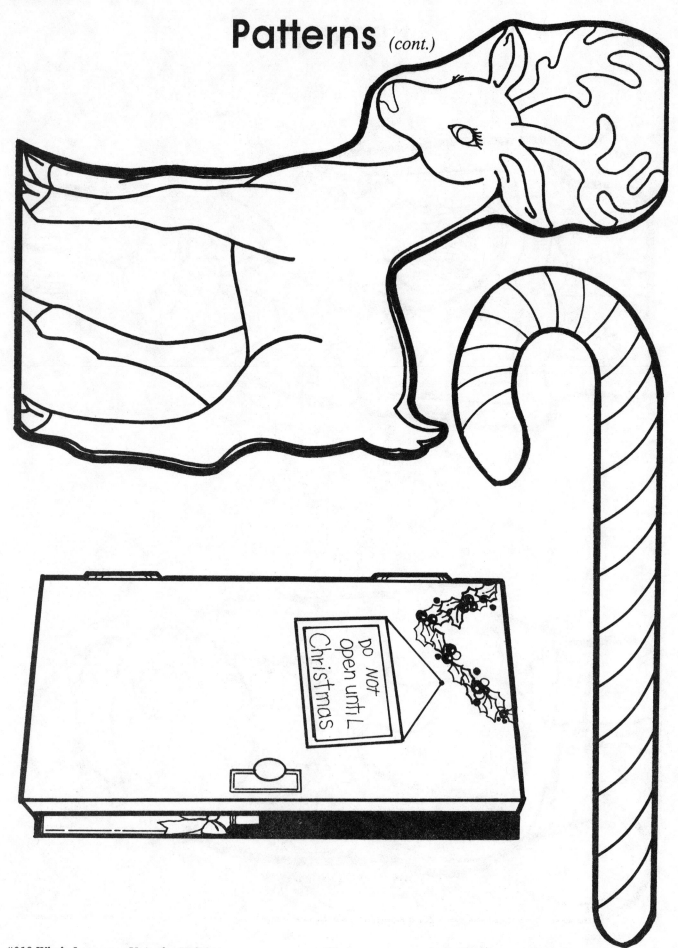

DO NOT
open until
Christmas

54

Patterns *(cont.)*

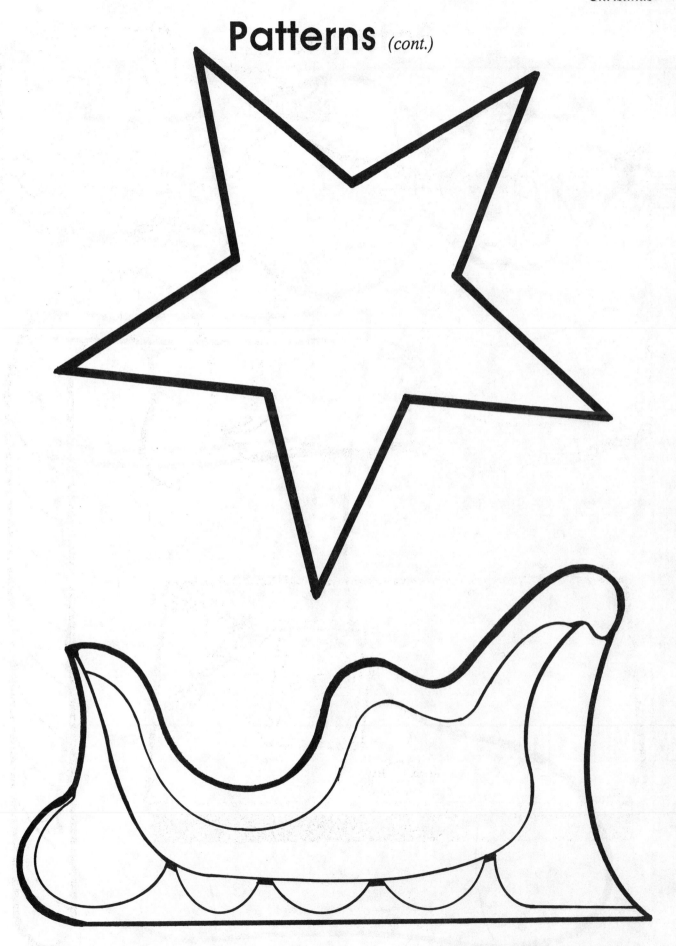

Patterns *(cont.)*

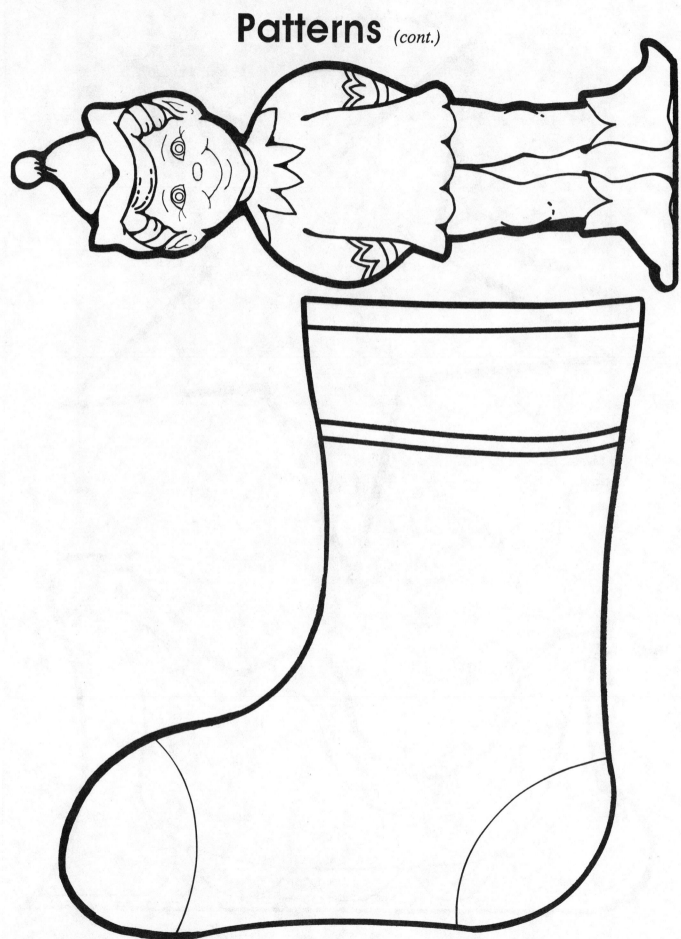

56

Patterns *(cont.)*

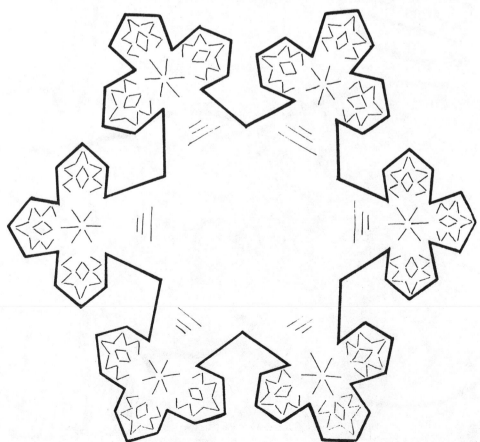

Patterns *(cont.)*

Patterns *(cont.)*

Patterns *(cont.)*

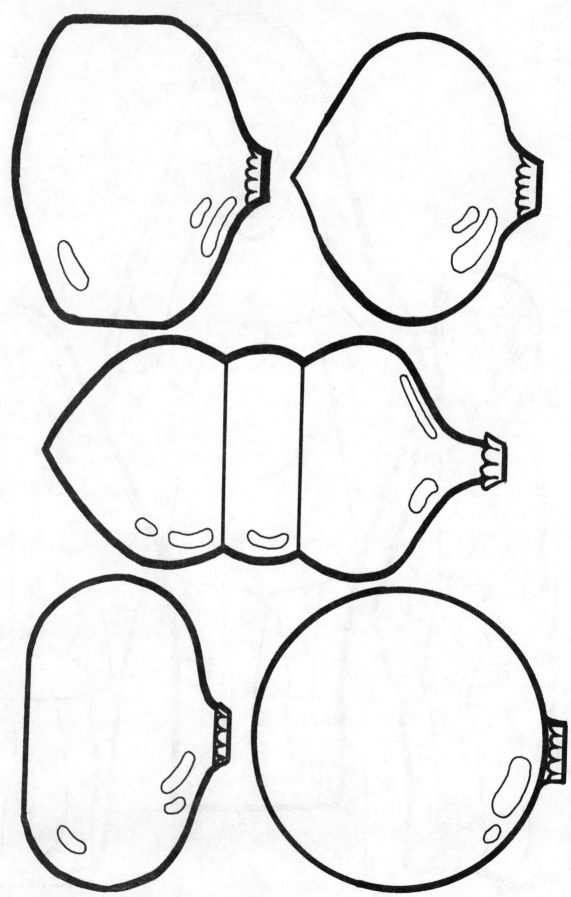

60

Christmas Riddles

Up on the rooftop,
Ho! Ho! Ho!
Little red suit
And a beard of snow.
Who am I? (Santa)

Use these riddles along with flannel board figures. They are an excellent way to teach inference to young children.

White as can be,
I can't run or play.
When the sun comes out,
I melt away.
What am I? (snowman)

It's almost Christmas.
I'm busy as a bee.
I help Santa make
All the toys, you see.
What am I? (elf)

Ribbons of stripes,
Red and white,
Great to eat,
A real delight.
What am I? (candy cane)

I have branches
And needles too,
Toys all around,
All shiny and new.
What am I? (tree)

I come your way
Before Christmas Day.
Merry Christmas
Is what I say.
What am I? (Christmas card)

Under the tree
Is where I'll be.
Wrapped in paper,
Fun to see.
What am I? (present)

Christmas Art Project

Color Santa's cap and clothing red. Glue cotton balls on his beard, hair, and hat.

Creative Writing

Add to the Little Books

Add a blank page at the end of the little books. Encourage the children to write and illustrate what they think happened next. Those not able to do this may simply write or copy and illustrate Christmas words on the blank page.

Two Letter Words

On the flannel board place Santa and an interfacing speech bubble (page 58) with the words: Ho, ho, ho! Explain speech bubbles by showing the children some newspaper comics. Use other speech bubbles to let Santa say some rhyming words like: go, so, no. Let the children copy. This exercise can also be done on the chalkboard.

All I Want for Christmas

During centers, work with a few children. Let them tell you what they want for Christmas. Have them cut out pictures from toy catalogues, circulars, and magazines. Glue the pictures onto a piece of paper. In front of each picture, help the child write, "I want a _____." creating a rebus letter. Some children may want to write the greeting, "Dear Santa," and sign their names.

Word Bank

A word bank is a collection of related words. It should grow and be added to as children learn more about the topic being studied. Suggested words for the word bank are taken from the holiday season and "Is It Christmas Yet?" Let children suggest additional words.

Use the words below to begin a Christmas word bank and word rings that students can contribute to as studies progress.

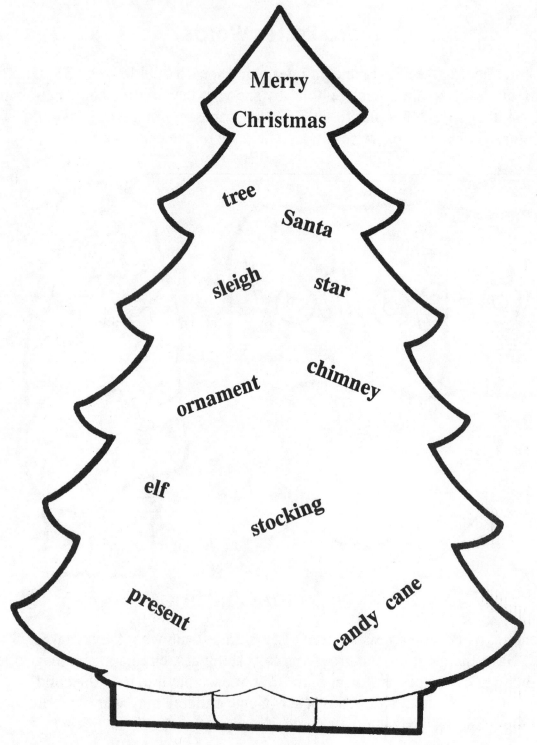

Making Little Books

My Little Book
of
Is It Christmas Yet?

_____
Name

One day I found a Christmas card.
"Mama! Mama!" I said,
"Is it Christmas yet?"
"Not yet," said Mama.
So I put it in the closet, and I waited.

1

Making Little Books *(cont.)*

One day I found a candy cane.
"Mama! Mama!" I said,
"Is it Christmas yet?"
"Not yet," said Mama.
So I put it in the closet, and I waited.   2

One day I found a Christmas present.
"Mama! Mama!" I said,
"Is it Christmas yet?"
"Not yet," said Mama.
So I put it in the closet, and I waited.   3

Making Little Books (cont.)

One day I found a Christmas tree.
"Mama! Mama!" I said,
"Is it Christmas yet?"
"Not yet," said Mama.
So I put it in the closet, and I waited.   4

One day I found a reindeer.
"Mama! Mama!" I said,
"Is it Christmas yet?"
"Not yet," said Mama.
So I put him in the closet, and I waited.   5

Making Little Books *(cont.)*

One day I found an elf.
"Mama! Mama!" I said,
"Is it Christmas yet?"
"Not yet," said Mama.
So I put him in the closet, and I waited.

6

One day I found Santa!
"Mama! Mama!" I said,
"Is it Christmas yet?"
"Yes," said Mama.

7

Making Little Books *(cont.)*

Out came the Christmas card.
Out came the candy cane.
Out came the Christmas present.
Out came the Christmas tree.
Out came the reindeer.
Out came the elf.

8

"Ho, ho, ho!" said Santa,
and it was Christmas!

9

"Is It Christmas Yet?"
Picture Match

Directions: Color the pictures. Cut on dotted lines. Glue the pictures beside the correct words.

Santa		
elf		
tree		
present		
Mama		

Christmas Tree Math

Make felt trees from the Christmas tree patterns on this page.

Let the children place them in order of size.

- Write numerals on each one and have children put them into correct number order.
- Create simple addition or subtraction problems by writing numerals on two trees. Have the answers on another set of trees for students to choose from.
- Make simple pattern sequences for children to match: e.g., big, big, little.
- Decorate them with small felt circles. Children count the number of ornaments.

Where Is Holly Heart?

"We need valentine cards for the school party," Megan said to Mark.
"Holly Heart said she would make some for us.
Let's go see Holly Heart."

They met Hoppy Heart.
"Holly Heart is not home," said Hoppy Heart.
"Let's go find her."

They met Dandy Dog.
"Have you seen Holly Heart?" they asked.
"No," said Dandy Dog.
"But I can show you a bone.
Do you want a bone?"
"No, thank you," they said.

They met Heart Bird.
"Have you seen Holly Heart?" they asked.
"No," said Heart Bird.
"But I can show you a worm.
Do you want a worm?"
"No, thank you," they said.

They met Buffy Butterfly.
"Have you seen Holly Heart?" they asked.
"No," said Buffy Butterfly.
"But I can show you a flower?
Do you want a flower?"
"No, thank you," they said.

72

Where is Holly Heart? *(cont.)*

They met Baby Heart.
"Have you seen Holly Heart?" they asked.
"Da, da, goo, goo," said Baby Heart.
"I can show you some toys.
Do you want to play?"
"No, thank you," they said.

They met the Love Bug.
"Have you seen Holly Heart?" they asked.
"I cannot talk," said the Love Bug.
"I am late for a valentine party."
"So are we," said Megan and Mark.
"And we don't have any valentines."
"Look," said Mark.
"This is Holly Heart's mailbox.
We are back where we started."

They heard a loud noise.
Thump, thump, thump!
The noise was coming from the mailbox!
Quickly, they opened the mailbox.
Out popped Holly Heart!

"The postman thought I was a valentine card," she said.
"He put me in the mailbox.
Thank you for saving me.
Here are your valentine cards."

Sample Lessons

Each of the lessons suggested can take from one to several days to complete.

Day 1: Put up a teaching bulletin board. Enlarge some of the patterns from "Where Is Holly Heart?" On each write its beginning sound in an upper case letter. Place on the bulletin board. Under each character attach a plastic strawberry basket, with a loop of ribbon and a tack. Make a set of hearts on colored poster board, tag, index, or wallpaper. On each heart write a lower case letter to match those on the bulletin board. Laminate. Place an extra basket to hold the hearts. Children place the hearts with the matching lower case letters in the baskets under the characters. To make this bulletin board more difficult, do not put letters on the bulletin board characters and write words on the hearts. Suggested words are: dog, baby, heart, Holly, Hoppy, butterfly, Mark, Megan, bird, mailbox, and valentine. Children match words to the characters.

Brainstorm before reading the story. Plan your class valentine party. Planning is a thinking skill that adults often use, but seldom discuss with children. Talk about what adults will need to provide: cookies, cupcakes, candy, plates, napkins, cups, drinks. Make a list on the board or chart as children make suggestions. Then talk about what the children will need to bring— valentines.

Read "Where Is Holly Heart?" Felt flannel board figures work best for this story. Place each character on the flannel board as they are introduced. If you don't have time to make flannel board figures, copy the characters on pink heavy stock, laminate, and tape to tongue depressors or craft sticks. Then put on a puppet show for your class. A table turned on its side can serve as a stage.

Day 2: Do some heart art. Children will be fascinated with the heart characters and will want to make some of their own. First they will need some practice tracing and drawing hearts of different sizes. You can make heart stencils several ways. The easiest way is to rip the lids and bottoms from boxes of valentine candy. Another method is to make a set of heart stencils by tracing around the patterns on page 83-85. If the children trace around the heart stencils on colored construction paper, they can cut them out and glue them to another piece of construction paper to make some heart art. Add faces, legs, etc., with crayons.

Sample Lessons *(cont.)*

Read "Where Is Holly Heart?" using a Big Book. Make the Big Book by printing each section of the story onto a separate, large piece of heavy paper. Duplicate, color, and cut out the appropriate character patterns from pages 77-81. Arrange and glue them to each page. Add a cover and bind with tape or rings. For a quick alternative, enlarge the little book (pages 87 to 91) on a copy machine. Assemble, add a cover, and bind into a Big Book.

Make a class book of "Where Is Holly Heart?" during center time. Work with a group of six to eight children. Provide a large number of construction paper scraps and pieces of construction paper. Discuss what pictures you will need and make a list: Mark, Megan, Holly, Hoppy, Dandy Dog, Love Bug, Baby Heart, Heart Bird, Buffy Butterfly. The children might also want to add a mailbox. Assign each child an art project. Use two pieces of poster board for the covers. Use tag or heavy art paper for the other pages. Help each child glue his/her character in the book. Pencil in the text and let the child trace over the text with a marker. Laminate and use the book again next year.

Day 3: Read the story again, this time emphasizing that the mail carrier confused Holly Heart with a valentine card. Show a picture of Holly Heart and let children guess how this might have happened.

Play post office. Choose a good book about the mail to read for motivation and vocabulary development. For example: *Special Delivery* by Betty Brandt (Carolrhoda, 1988) or *The Jolly Postman* by Janet and Allan Ahlberg (Little, 1986) Extend into learning addresses, reading maps, finding house numbers, and looking at mail. Teach the children to make an envelope by folding and gluing a piece of manila. Have them write their names and addresses (if appropriate) on the envelopes. If you save stamps from junk mail (like the stamps from magazine promotions), the children can put a "play stamp" on the envelope. Emphasize that these are not real stamps, and explain that real stamps come from the post office. Children can make word cards, valentine cards, or write "letters" to put in the envelopes.

Sample Lessons *(cont.)*

Day 4: Make little books (pages 87-91) of "Where is Holly Heart?" Let children color them. (See page 6 for assembly). Children can read the books as you read the story to them.

Complete a valentine math activity (page 92).

Let children "play" the story. Create Holly Heart's house as a special valentine center. Holly and Hoppy Heart pillows are easy to make. Cut and sew heart shaped felt and stuff with cotton. Faces can be drawn with a marker or glue on colored felt pieces. Unless you are good at sewing, leave off arms, legs, and clothes; just make the faces. Sew on Holly Heart's bows. Save some old valentines for the children to play with. A doll can be Baby Heart, and a stuffed dog can be Dandy Dog. If you have other stuffed animals that weren't in the story, encourage the children to make up parts for them. Say, "What would a lion say? Would he show them some meat?" Ask the children to "rewrite the story" and put themselves in it. They can use their own names or make up new names.

Day 5: As a culminating activity hold the valentine party that students helped to organize on the first day of the unit. Point out the connections between what they have organized and the party they are enjoying. Invite another class. Play the King or Queen of Hearts game (see pages 83-84) and read the little books to them.

Patterns

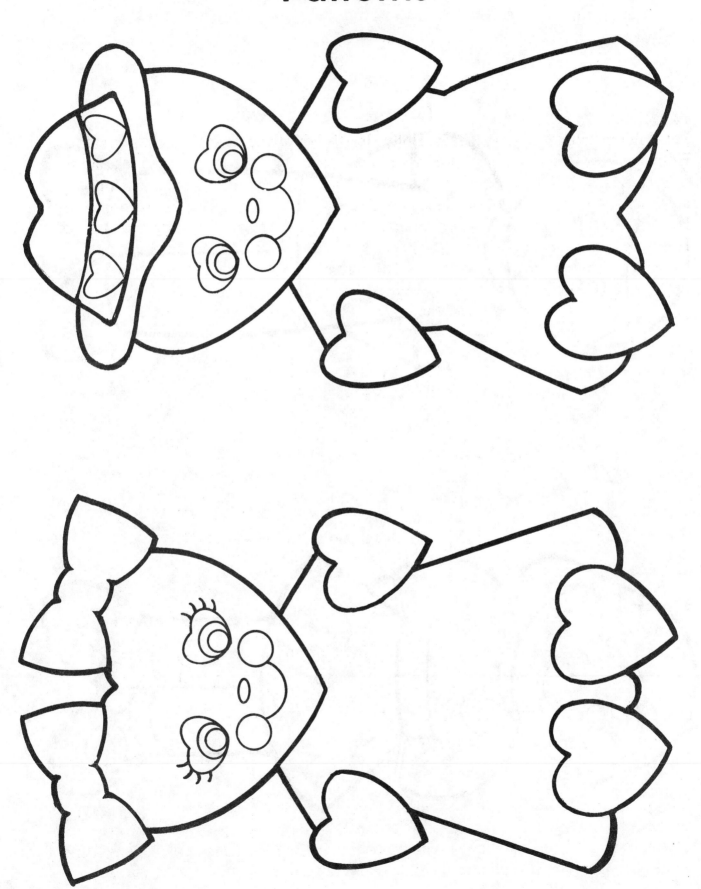

Patterns *(cont.)*

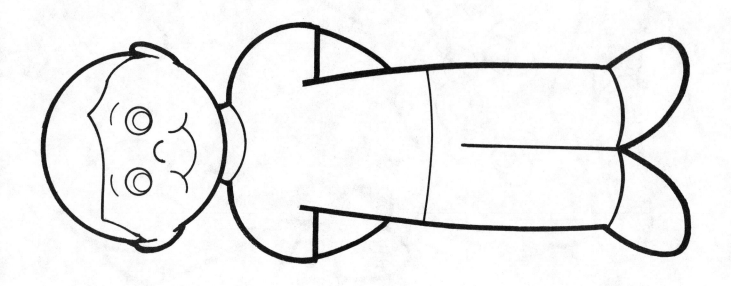

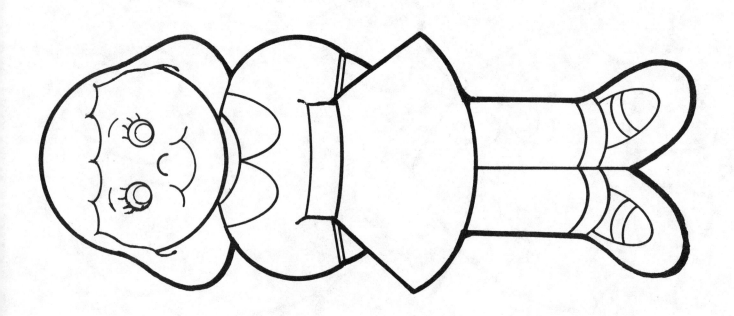

78

Patterns *(cont.)*

Patterns *(cont.)*

Patterns *(cont.)*

Valentine Riddles

Read some valentine riddles. After the children give the answer, write the correct word on the chalkboard.

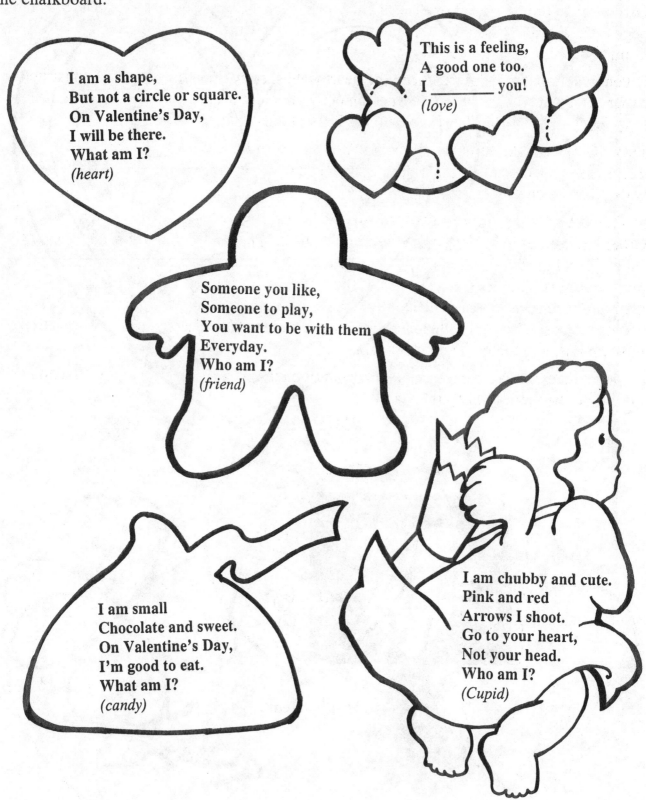

I am a shape,
But not a circle or square.
On Valentine's Day,
I will be there.
What am I?
(heart)

This is a feeling,
A good one too.
I _____ you!
(love)

Someone you like,
Someone to play,
You want to be with them
Everyday.
Who am I?
(friend)

I am small
Chocolate and sweet.
On Valentine's Day,
I'm good to eat.
What am I?
(candy)

I am chubby and cute.
Pink and red
Arrows I shoot.
Go to your heart,
Not your head.
Who am I?
(Cupid)

82

The King or Queen of Hearts

Children will have fun playing this Valentine game while practicing phonics skills.

Directions: To make a set of heart wands for the teacher to keep, use the patterns on this page and page 84. Reproduce them onto colored construction paper or colored index. Laminate and tape to tongue depressors or craft sticks.

If you wish to let the children keep the heart wands, copy them onto colored construction paper. Get some of the students who can cut well to cut them during centers or when they finish their work. Then staple all the hearts to drinking straws.

Play: Children take turns being the King of Hearts or the Queen of Hearts. The king/queen takes a basket of heart wands and walks around a circle of children. As he/she walks, he/she chants:

As I slowly walk around, tell me the beginning sound.

Other children or the teacher may join in the chant. The king/queen stops on the word "sound" and gives a heart wand to the nearest child. If the child can tell what letter the picture begins with, he/she gets to hold the wand. If not, he/she gives the wand back and the king/queen walks again. The king/ queen continues around and around until all the wands are passed out. The teacher then chooses a new king/queen, usually one with the most wands, and the game begins again.

To make the game harder, put words instead of pictures on the heart wands. The child must read the word to keep the wand.

Patterns

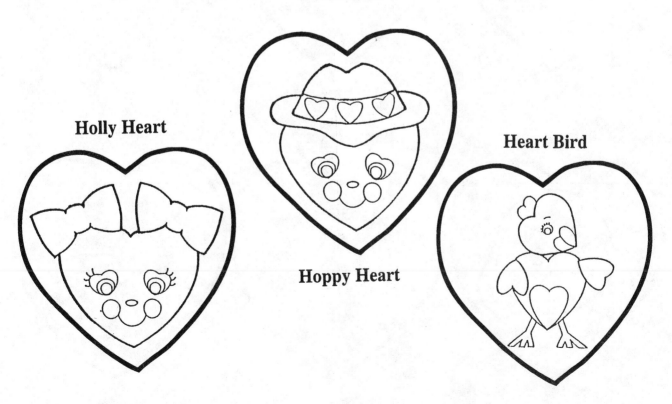

Holly Heart

Hoppy Heart

Heart Bird

The King or Queen of Hearts *(cont.)*

valentine

dog

bug

mailbox

butterfly

Mark

Megan

Baby Heart

candy

84

Word Bank

A word bank is a collection of related words. It should grow and be added to as children learn more about the topic being studied. Suggested words for the word bank are taken from the holiday season and "Where Is Holly Heart?" Let children suggest additional words. Use the words to make word rings. (See directions on page 4.)

Use the heart shape that contains the words as a template for creating art projects.

Suggested Words for Valentine Word Bank

Creative Writing

Make a Valentine

Provide red and pink construction paper, pre-cut hearts, paper lace, stickers, etc. Give a lesson in paper cutting: scallops, frames, heart flowers, negative hearts. (See page 81.) Let students design their own valentine cards.

Instead of a preprinted verse, have students copy "I love you." from the chalkboard. Older children may be able to compose their own messages. Don't forget that, "I luv yoo." and "I luv u." are accepted spellings when students attempt to write words without adult help. Tell them, "Just sound them out and spell the best you can."

Friendship

Valentine's Day is about romantic love, but for youngsters, it's about friendship. Talk about what it means to be a friend. Young children are also very interested in how to make friends. Then combine cloze with creative writing. Place name cards in a pocket chart or list student's names on the chalkboard. Write "I like _____." on the chalkboard as a model. Students complete by adding classmate's names. (A good way to include all children is to put all the children's names in a box and have students each choose one.) Provide a photocopy of individual photos of the whole class for each student to cut out and glue on. Older students can add thoughts about friendship or write what they like about their friends.

Baby Heart Speaks

Many children need a gentle nudge to start spelling words without a grownup's help. Since Baby Heart sometimes speaks in baby talk, he can encourage risk taking. Talk about what Baby Heart would say. He might say "Mom" or "Dad" or he might just speak in jibberish. Show students how to make cartoon speech bubbles. Then give everyone a precut red construction paper heart to make Baby Heart. Let students glue it onto a large piece of manila. Then add facial features, hands, and feet with crayons. Tell them to write what Baby Heart says. It's impossible to make a mistake bacause Baby Heart can make any kind of sound or talk in nonsense words. Most students will also want to add other characters like Dandy Dog and Love Bug and let them talk too.

Imagination

Children can use the flannel board in the reading center to make up more Holly Heart stories. Help the children with a story starter: Holly Heart was planning a valentine party. Ask students to make up a story about Holly Heart at the grocery store buying the things for her party. Would her pets go with her? Would they get into trouble? They can use small felt hearts to represent cakes, cookies, or plates. Students can write their stories later. Younger students can draw story pictures in panels (cartoon style) instead of writing a story.

Making Little Books

My Little Book
of
Where Is Holly Heart?

_____

Name

"We need valentine cards for the school party," Megan said to Mark.
"Holly Heart said she would make some for us. Let's go see Holly Heart."

Making Little Books

1

Making Little Books

They met Hoppy Heart.
"Holly Heart is not home," said Hoppy Heart.
"Let's go find her."

2

They met Dandy Dog.
"Have you seen Holly Heart?" they asked.
"No," said Dandy Dog.
"But I can show you a bone.
Do you want a bone?"
"No, thank you," they said.

3

Making Little Books

They met Heart Bird.
"Have you seen Holly Heart?" they asked.
"No," said Heart Bird.
"But I can show you a worm.
Do you want a worm?"
"No, thank you," they said.

4

They met Buffy Butterfly.
"Have you seen Holly Heart?" they asked.
"No," said Buffy Butterfly.
"But I can show you a flower?
Do you want a flower?"
"No, thank you," they said.

5

Making Little Books

They met Baby Heart.
"Have you seen Holly Heart?" they asked.
"Da, da, goo, goo," said Baby Heart.
"I can show you some toys.
Do you want to play?"
"No, thank you," they said.

6

They met the Love Bug.
"Have you seen Holly Heart?" they asked.
"I cannot talk," said the Love Bug.
"I am late for a valentine party."
"So are we," said Megan and Mark.
"And we don't have any valentines."

7

    90

Making Little Books

"Look," said Mark. "This is Holly Heart's mailbox. We are back where we started."
They heard a loud noise. Thump, thump, thump!
The noise was coming from the mailbox!
Quickly, they opened the mailbox.
Out popped Holly Heart!

8

"The postman thought I was a valentine card," she said.
"He put me in the mailbox.
Thank you for saving me.
Here are your valentines."

HAPPY VALENTINE

9

Valentine Math

Use the valentine patterns, pages 77-81, to make characters for the math problems. The characters are the same as the characters in the little book. You will also need about 10 small hearts for the flannel board to be valentines, cookies, and plates.

Holly Heart Stories

Holly Heart invited 3 people to her party: Hoppy, Mark, and Megan. How many people were at Holly's party? (Clue: Don't forget to count Holly.) Put up characters to show the 4 people.

Using Holly Heart characters, let students solve these problems.

Holly Heart's mother gave her 6 new heart-shaped plates to use at her party. There were 4 people at the party (Holly, Hoppy, Mark, Megan). Were there more plates or more people? Match plates to people to show which is more. Explain.

Baby Heart was too young to go to the party. Holly and Hoppy gave him valentines instead. How many valentines did Baby Heart get? Match valentines to Hoppy and Holly; give to Baby.

Baby Heart was still crying because he didn't get to go to the party. Holly said she would give him some cookies after the party. She gave Hoppy 3 leftover cookies, and she gave Baby Heart 4 leftover cookies. Baby Heart kept crying. He said, "Hoppy has more cookies, and I have less." Was he right? Can you match to see who has more and who has less?

Holly wanted to give some leftover cookies to her pets: Dandy Dog, Buffy Butterfly, Heart Bird, and Love Bug. How many cookies will she need? Put out a large stack of hearts and ask a child to match the heart cookies to the pets, one for each pet.

Hearts In Order

Make 10 small hearts on smooth interfacing material. Using a permanent fine point marker, write the numerals 1 through 10 on the hearts. Color the hearts with a red or pink crayon. Tell the children to mix the hearts and then try to put them in order on the flannel board.

Missing Hearts

The teacher places hearts from the activity above in numerical order on the flannel board. Students turn around while the teacher removes one or more hearts. Then they try to guess which heart is missing and put it back in the correct position.

Easter Bunny School

"I love school," said Betty Bunny,
and she rode the Bunny School bus.

"I love school," said Rhonda Rabbit,
and she mixed the paint.

"I love school," said Bobby Bunny,
and he painted the eggs.

"I love school," said Ricky Rabbit,
and he fixed the baskets.

"I love school," said Bobby Bunny,
and he hid the eggs.

"I love school," said Rhonda Rabbit,
and she ate the Bunny School lunch.

"I love school," said Betty Bunny,
and she did the bunny hop.

"I love school," said Ricky Rabbit,
"And I will come back tomorrow."

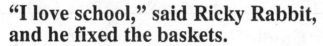
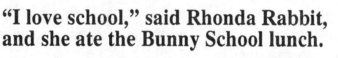

Sample Lessons

Each of the lessons suggested can take from one to several days to complete.

Note: Before presenting the unit prepare flannel board patterns. The patterns in this unit lend themselves to being copied onto wallpaper. See page 5 for ways to do this.

Day 1: Before reading "Easter Bunny School," make it into a Big Book. (See page 6 for directions.) Read the book just for enjoyment without stopping. Reread, using a pointer. Encourage the children to join in on the second reading.

After reading "Easter Bunny School" twice, ask what other things young rabbits might do or learn at a school for Easter bunnies. Answers might include getting eggs from chickens, putting stickers on eggs, hopping in bunny races, making candy bunnies, and putting jelly beans in the baskets. If children have trouble coming up with answers, do some research. Read *Happy Easter* by Kurt Wiese (Penguin, 1989).

Make wallpaper eggs. Before the lesson make an egg stencil (page 99) for each student in the class. Talk about creating Easter pictures. Some possibilities include scenes from "Easter Bunny School," children hunting eggs, or a basket with eggs. Have students cut strips from wallpaper sample books (often available from decorating and wallpaper stores). Show them how to trace and cut out an egg. Give each child a large piece of manila or construction paper and glue. Using pencils, crayons, and the wallpaper eggs, have each create an Easter scene.

Day 2: Make transparencies of the little book pages and present the story on the overhead. Help the children look for repetition. Underline the repeated words and phrases with an overhead marker. Make a list of repeated words. Use later with word cards.

Use the riddles on page 102 and the flannel board figures. After the children give the answer to each riddle, place the correct Easter figure on the flannel board. Add an interfacing word card to review each Easter word.

Using words such as rabbit, bunny, paint, eggs, basket, lunch, hop, school, duck, lamb, candy, bird, and nest, make Easter word rings. See page 4 for directions. Use them in centers. (See page 7.)

Sample Lessons *(cont.)*

Day 3: Take the sentences from " Easter Bunny School" and make sentence strips of the story for use in a pocket chart. Present the story in the pocket chart. The wallpaper or tag flannel board figures do nicely in a pocket chart too. They can be placed beside the sentence strips.

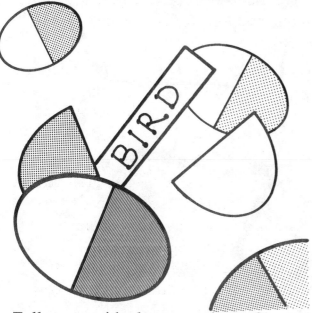

Obtain plastic Easter eggs that open. Put one Easter interfacing word card inside each egg. Place the Easter figures on the flannel board. Put the eggs in a basket (or other container). Let one student be the Easter Bunny and pass out eggs to the students one at a time. As each student opens his/her egg, let him/her come up and match the word card to the correct Easter figure on the flannel board. Those who cannot read the word can say the beginning letter and make the sound of that letter. The teacher may prompt by saying, "Do you see anything that begins with 'b' on the flannel board?"

Follow up with cloze exercises. Cloze simply means missing word or words. Copy part of "Easter Bunny School" on the chalkboard.

Example: "I _____ _____," said Rhonda _____, and she rode the Bunny School _____. Have children supply the missing words.

Day 4: Read the story, putting characters up on the flannel board. Use the characters to help complete word story problems that you create or to complete problems on page 110.

Do the "Easter Bunny School" picture match on page 109 or the sequencing exercise on page 112. To make a set of Egg Sequencing cards for teacher or center use, enlarge page 112, copy on heavy stock, cut, color, and laminate. Cards may be sequenced on a chalkboard ledge.

Extend the story into holiday centers (page 7). Let students make little books, illustrating the cover.

Day 5: Let students present the story chorally. In small groups have them read different pages using their little books as "scripts."

As a culminating activity, decorate Easter eggs with your class by painting them as they do in "Easter Bunny School." Use hard-boiled or blown-out eggs and let students use water colors or tempera paints. Hide the eggs for an egg hunt.

Patterns

Patterns *(cont.)*

Patterns *(cont.)*

Patterns *(cont.)*

Patterns (cont.)

Patterns *(cont.)*

Easter Riddles

Use these riddles along with flannel board figures. They are an excellent way to teach inference to young children.

I'm so sweet and fun to eat.
I may be your favorite treat.
What am I?
(candy)

Different colors,
Oval and bright,
Hidden in the grass
On Easter night,
Children hunt me
In the morning light.
What am I?
(egg)

On Easter, I can't be found.
But you know I've been around.
I bring surprises, good to eat.
I have long ears and big, big feet.
What am I?
(rabbit)

High in a tree,
Just made of twigs,
Babies live here,
Till they get big.
What am I?
(nest)

Filled with candy eggs,
Buy me at the store.
I carry eggs
When you hunt for more.
What am I?
(basket)

I have bright feathers.
My song is sweet.
I think a worm
Is good to eat.
What am I?
(bird)

Far out in space,
So hot and bright,
I shine in the sky,
But not at night.
What am I?
(sun)

102

Creative Writing

New Stories from Old

Use the word pattern from "Easter Bunny School" to help children write about their school experiences. Let the class brainstorm as many school activities as possible. Record them on the chalkboard and read over them. Choose the best ones to put in a class book. Use the children's names in the blank:

"I love school," said _____, and he/she *rode the school bus*.

Other phrases to replace the italicized words might include:

- read a book
- painted a picture
- ate her lunch
- went to the library
- played outside
- sang a song
- did his math problems
- worked on the computer

Add the ending line, putting your name in the blank. "School is over," said Ms./Mr. ___, and she/he went home.

Making a Class Book

Begin with two poster boards. Cut each into four pieces so that there are eight pieces in all. On the cover, write the title "I Love School." Brainstorm with the children about what they love about school. Let students draw school scenes suggested in the brainstorming session on sheets of drawing paper. Color with crayons, chalk, or watercolor. Glue the drawings on the posterboard pieces. Write the text on each page with a pencil. The student author of that page traces over the teacher's words with a fine point marker. Leave a blank for each child's name. Laminate the pages. Students can write their names with erasable marker so the book can then be used again next year by writing in new student names.

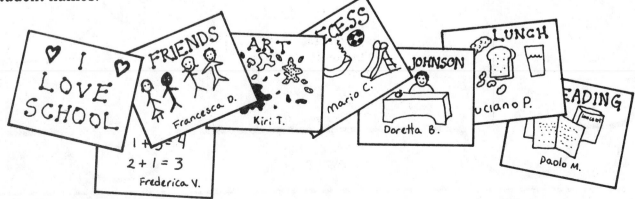

- -

My Little Book
of
Easter Bunny School

_____

Name

- -

"I love school," said Betty Bunny,
and she rode the Bunny School bus.

1

Making Little Books *(cont.)*

"I love school," said Rhonda Rabbit, and she mixed the paint.

2

"I love school," said Bobby Bunny, and he painted the eggs.

3

Making Little Books

"I love school," said
Ricky Rabbit,
and he fixed the
baskets.

4

"I love school," said
Bobby Bunny,
and he hid the eggs.

5

Making Little Books

"I love school," said
Rhonda Rabbit,
and she ate the Bunny
School lunch.

6

"I love school," said
Betty Bunny,
and she did the bunny
hop.

7

Making Little Books

"I love school," said
Ricky Rabbit,
"And I will come back
tomorrow."

8

The End

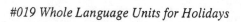

"Easter Bunny School" Picture Match

Directions: Color pictures. Cut on dotted lines. Glue the pictures beside the correct words.

eggs		
rabbit		
basket		
bus		
hop		

Easter Egg Math

Directions: This is a good whole class activity. Copy page 111 for each child. If your copier has the ability to enlarge, copy the picture on legal size paper. Children can color the paper before using it for math. It might be better to do the coloring on one day and the math on another day. You will need manipulatives for this activity. Jelly beans are a fun manipulative (beans, counters, or paper clips can also be used). Let the children use them for eggs on the picture. As you read the problem, have the children place the jelly beans on the picture and answer orally. When they finish with math, they can eat the jelly beans. To make it even more fun, place a flannel board figure on the flannel board with the correct number of eggs as you read each problem.

Addition Problems

1. Bobby Bunny hid Easter eggs. He hid 1 in front of the house and 1 beside the big tree. How many eggs did he hide?

2. A playful cat saw the bunnies hiding eggs and decided to move them. He put 2 eggs in the flowers and 1 egg near a bush. How many eggs did he move? (Use the cat page 11 for the playful cat.)

3. The bunnies were upset when they found out their eggs had been moved. They called Rhonda Rabbit to help. She found 2 eggs in the grass and 1 egg high in the tree. How many eggs did she find?

4. Baby Duck wanted to hunt eggs. Her mom said she was too little because she had just hatched. But Baby Duck found 2 eggs in the window of the house and 2 eggs beside the house. How many eggs did she find?

5. Baby Bunny was too young to hide eggs, but he could hunt them. He found 1 egg in the flowers and 2 eggs beside the house. How many eggs did he find?

6. Betty Bunny wanted to hunt eggs, too, but they were too easy to find. She called the magic bunny to hide the eggs in impossible places. The magic bunny hid 2 eggs in the clouds and 2 eggs in the rainbow. How many eggs did the magic bunny hide? (Use Ricky Rabbit figure for the magic bunny.)

Easter Egg Math *(cont.)*

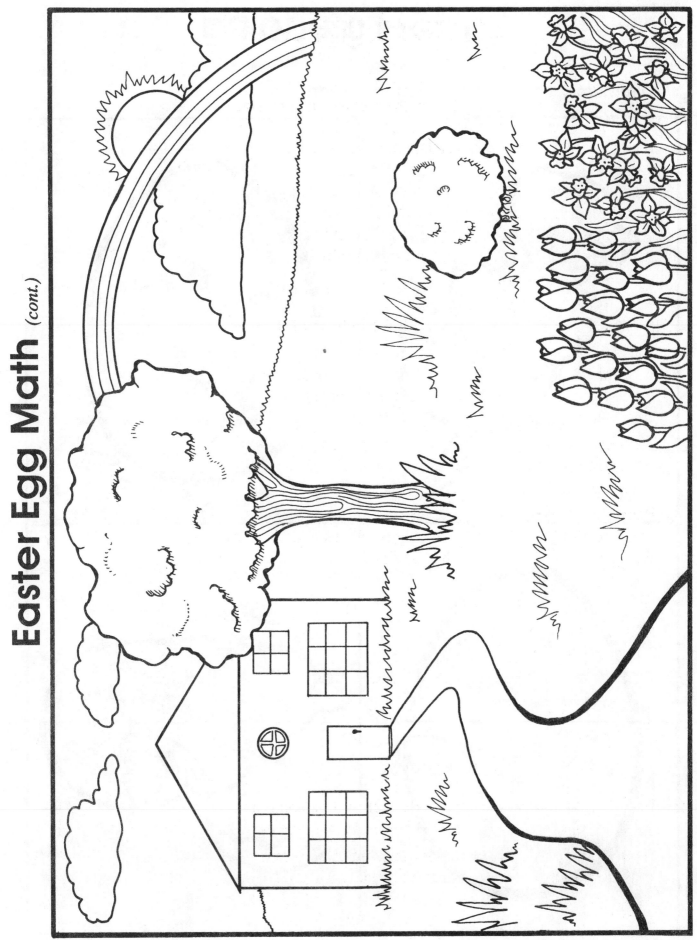

Egg Sequencing

Directions: Color, cut and place in order.